The Psychology of Inquiry

Understanding the Scientific Method in Psychology

Freudian Trips

Copyright Page

Disclaimer

The views and opinions expressed in this book are those of the author(s) and do not necessarily reflect the official policy or position of any other agency, organization, employer, or company. The contents of this book are for informational and educational purposes only and are not intended to serve as professional advice, diagnosis, or treatment.

The information provided in this book is believed to be accurate and reliable as of the date of publication. However, it may include some errors or inaccuracies, and no warranty or guarantee is provided regarding the accuracy, timeliness, or applicability of the content.

Readers are encouraged to consult with professional philosophers, educators, or other qualified professionals where appropriate for personalized advice. The author(s) and publisher shall not be liable for any loss, damage, or harm caused or alleged to be caused, directly or indirectly, by the information or ideas contained, suggested, or referenced in this book.

By reading this book, the reader acknowledges and agrees that they are solely responsible for how they interpret and apply the information contained herein.

This book may also include references to other works, studies, and sources. These references are provided for further reading and exploration and do not imply endorsement or validation of the specific theories, viewpoints, or interpretations presented in those works.

Chapter 1: Introduction to the Scientific Method in Psychology

Imagine you're baking a cake for the first time. You'd likely follow a specific recipe, measuring each ingredient carefully and following each step in order. If you veer off the recipe, you might end up with something entirely different! The scientific method is a bit like that recipe. It's a set of steps that researchers follow to understand the world around us accurately. Just as in baking, if you skip a step or don't measure correctly, you might not get the results you were expecting.

Understanding the Scientific Method

The scientific method is a systematic way of investigating questions and discovering new knowledge. It's not just limited to people in white lab coats; it's a logical process that we all use in our daily lives, often without even realizing it! Think of the last time you lost your keys. You probably had a theory about where they might be, looked there, and based on whether you found them or not, came up with a new theory. That's the scientific method in action!

In its most basic form, the scientific method involves:

Observing something interesting or puzzling.

Asking questions about what you've observed.

Formulating a possible answer or hypothesis.

Testing that hypothesis through experiments.

Analyzing the results to see if your hypothesis was correct.

Repeating the process to make sure the results are consistent.

The Role of the Scientific Method in Psychology

Now, you might be wondering, "What does baking or lost keys have to do with psychology?" Psychology is, after all, the study of behavior and the mind. Psychologists apply the scientific method to research thoughts, attitudes, and behaviors in the same way that bakers use recipes to make cakes.

Imagine you're curious about why some people are more outgoing than others. A psychologist might use the scientific method to test the theory that early childhood experiences influence this trait. They'd gather data, conduct experiments, and analyze the results to gain a better understanding. Without the scientific method, we'd be left relying on guesses or assumptions, which isn't very reliable!

Importance of Empirical Evidence

One of the key aspects of the scientific method is the reliance on empirical evidence. "Empirical" might sound like a fancy word, but it just means information that is based on observation or experience rather than theory or pure logic. In other words, it's evidence you can see, touch, and measure.

Let's go back to our cake analogy. Suppose you tell a friend that adding more sugar to the cake recipe will make it sweeter. That's just a theory until you actually try it. Once you bake the cake with more sugar and taste it, you have empirical evidence that your theory was right (or wrong)!

In psychology, empirical evidence ensures that the conclusions drawn are based on real-world observations and experiments rather than just personal beliefs or opinions. This makes the findings more reliable and trustworthy.

In summary, the scientific method is a tried-and-true recipe for understanding our world, including the complexities of the human mind and behavior. By following its steps and relying on empirical evidence, psychology can provide insights that are both meaningful and accurate. So, the next time you're curious about why people act the way they do or how the mind works, remember the role of the scientific method in guiding those answers!

Chapter 2: Tracing the Origins: The Scientific Method in Psychology

Imagine embarking on a journey through a vast and intricate tapestry, woven with threads of curiosity, discovery, and brilliance. This tapestry represents the history of psychology and its union with the scientific method. Let's explore this landscape together, discovering how the discipline we know today has been shaped over time.

A Glimpse into History

The story of psychology doesn't start in a modern-day lab with beeping machines and computers. No, it takes us back to ancient civilizations, where thinkers pondered the nature of the human mind and behavior. The Greeks, for instance, had their own thoughts about human temperament, categorizing people based on "humors" or body fluids. While this might sound strange now, it was an early attempt to systematically understand human behavior.

Fast forward a few centuries, and we see the birth of modern psychology. It began as a branch of philosophy, with scholars questioning consciousness, perception, and emotion. But as the years progressed, there was a shift. Instead of just pondering and speculating, individuals began to seek concrete evidence for their theories.

Luminaries and Their Legacies

As we stroll through this historical tapestry, certain figures stand out, their contributions acting as guiding stars in the vast sky of psychological inquiry.

Wilhelm Wundt: Often called the "father of modern psychology," Wundt opened the first psychology laboratory in Leipzig, Germany, in 1879. He believed in studying the mind using introspection, where individuals reported their conscious experiences.

William James: Across the ocean in America, James was pioneering his own path. His book, "Principles of Psychology," explored a wide range of topics and is still influential today. He believed in understanding the function of behaviors and thoughts, asking not just what they are, but why they exist.

John Watson: Watson ushered in a new era, known as behaviorism. He believed that psychology should focus on observable behaviors, not the murky waters of consciousness. For Watson, if it couldn't be seen or measured, it wasn't worth studying.

These are just a few of the brilliant minds that have shaped psychology. Each brought their own perspective, adding a unique thread to the tapestry.

The Evolving Path of Inquiry

The scientific method in psychology hasn't been a static entity. Like a river, it has meandered and evolved, reflecting the changing landscapes of society and scientific understanding.

In the early days, introspection was the primary tool. But as we've seen with figures like Watson, there was a shift towards observable behaviors. The latter half of the 20th century brought another change, with a renewed interest in cognition, the processes of the mind.

Technological advancements, like brain imaging, have further refined the scientific method in psychology. Today, we can peek into the brain, seeing which areas light up during different tasks or emotions. This fusion of biology and psychology, known as neuroscience, represents the exciting frontier of the discipline.

From ancient philosophers to modern neuroscientists, the quest to understand the human mind and behavior has been a thrilling journey. The scientific method, with its emphasis on evidence and systematic inquiry, has been the compass guiding this exploration. As we look back, we appreciate the pioneers of the past and eagerly anticipate the discoveries of the future.

Chapter 3: Baking Up the Scientific Method

When it comes to whipping up some psychological insights, the scientific method is like a tried-and-true recipe. But before we can bake up our latest behavioral experiment, we need high quality ingredients. Let's walk through gathering those step-by-step:

Identifying a Research Problem

Every master chef starts by surveying their pantry. What ingredients do they have to work with? What problems need solving? Psychologists similarly start by identifying phenomena that need explanation. For example, why do some memories fade quickly while others solidify? By clearly defining the research problem, we know where to focus our efforts.

Conducting a Literature Review

Before developing a new recipe, chefs will often research what others have done. Have similar ingredients been combined before? What worked and what didn't? Psychologists also review previous research to build on existing knowledge. Examining other memory studies might reveal useful theories or methodologies we can incorporate.

Formulating a Hypothesis

With ingredients and research in hand, chefs will propose a recipe they think will work. Psychologists do the same by forming hypotheses about what might be causing the phenomenon under investigation. For instance, perhaps memories formed under stress fade more quickly. The hypothesis gives us something specific to test.

Designing the Experiment

Now it's time to map out how we'll test our hypothesis. Chefs plan how to combine and cook the ingredients. Psychologists design studies to see if the hypothesis holds up. Key factors like sample size, variables, and methods must be determined.

Collecting and Analyzing Data

Once the cake goes into the oven, chefs carefully observe outcomes. Do they see the rise and textures they expected? Psychologists collect data and analyze results from the experiment to see if they support the original hypothesis. Statistical tests help interpret the findings.

Interpreting and Reporting Results

After pulling a cake from the oven, chefs must decide if it turned out as intended. Did that new frosting recipe work? Similarly, psychologists interpret data to determine whether results align with the hypothesis or if a new theory is needed. Findings are then reported in scientific publications.

And there you have it - the step-by-step method for whipping up psychological studies. While the scientific process involves more meticulous measuring and testing than baking, the basic ingredients are the same - careful preparation, precision, and a whole lot of patience waiting for the "cake" to be done. Bon appétit!

Chapter 4: Unraveling the Puzzle: Key Concepts of the Scientific Method

Picture yourself trying to complete a massive jigsaw puzzle. Each piece represents a unique element of a broader picture, and every one of them is essential to see the full image. The scientific method in psychology is a bit like this puzzle, with several key components fitting together to create a coherent understanding of human behavior and the mind. Let's dive into these foundational pieces and see how they contribute to the bigger picture.

The Magic of Variables

Imagine you're trying to find out if listening to calming music can reduce stress. The type of music (calming or not) would be something you can change or control. This is called an "independent variable." The level of stress you're measuring, which may change based on the music, is the "dependent variable."

In simpler terms, variables are like the ingredients in a recipe. Change an ingredient (like using spicy sauce instead of mild), and the final dish (like the spiciness of the meal) changes. In our experiments, we tweak one thing (independent variable) to see if it causes a change in something else (dependent variable).

The Unsung Heroes: Control Groups

Let's stick with our music example. If you want to see if calming music reduces stress, you'd have one group of people listen to calming music. But how do you know it's the music causing any changes and not something else, like just taking a break?

Enter the control group! This group might sit in silence or listen to neutral sounds. By comparing the two groups, we can be more confident that any changes in stress levels are due to the calming music and not other factors.

Think of the control group as our "baseline" or "comparison group." It's like tasting a dish before adding any spices to know the difference the spices make.

The Fairness Factor: Randomization

Imagine you're picking teams for a game. If one team gets all the strong players and the other all the novices, it wouldn't be a fair match. Randomization is like picking team members out of a hat. It ensures that each group in an experiment is comparable, making the results more trustworthy.

In our music experiment, we'd want to make sure both our music listeners and our control group have a mix of people—old, young, stressed, relaxed—to ensure one group doesn't have an advantage.

The Power of Statistical Significance

Here's a tricky one, but stick with me! Let's say you've tried two different brands of plant food to see which makes your flowers bloom more. After a month, the flowers with Brand A have two more blooms than those with Brand B. Does this mean Brand A is better?

Not so fast! What if it was just a fluke? Statistical significance is a way of figuring out if our results, like the two extra blooms, are likely due to the changes we made (using Brand A) or if they could have happened by chance.

In simpler terms, it's like checking if a coin is biased. If you flip it 10 times and get 7 heads, you might wonder. But if you flip it 1000 times and get 700 heads, you'd be more convinced there's something up with that coin.

So there we have it! Like puzzle pieces, these concepts – variables, control groups, randomization, and statistical significance – fit together to form the bigger picture of the scientific method in psychology. Understanding these components helps us appreciate the intricacy and rigor of the experiments and studies that shape our knowledge of the human mind.

Chapter 5: Taste-Testing the Scientific Method

Now that we've gone over the basic ingredients and steps of the scientific method recipe, let's take a taste to see how it comes together. Psychology has cooked up some classic studies that give us a flavor of the scientific method in action:

Pavlov's Classical Conditioning

Ivan Pavlov discovered that dogs drool at the sound of a tone associated with food. His controlled experiments identified conditioning as the reason behind this salivating response. Like a chef systematically testing ingredients, Pavlov used scientific methods to uncover the mechanics of learning.

Milgram's Obedience Study

Imagine a chef making a shocking discovery that people will obey authority even if it harms others. Stanley Milgram's controversial experiments revealed just that. He tested his hypothesis using measurable data, analysis, and rigorous methodology. His research shed light on a disturbing human tendency.

Loftus' Studies on Eyewitness Testimony

Through carefully designed experiments, Elizabeth Loftus showed how easily memories can be altered or distorted. Like a chef remixing a recipe, her work demonstrated how outside factors can modify our recollection. This research illuminated the malleability of memory using tested scientific methods.

Zimbardo's Stanford Prison Experiment

Philip Zimbardo randomly assigned volunteers to be "prisoners" or "guards" to see what would happen. Things got out of hand quickly, and the experiment was ended early. Like an unstable new recipe, the study design had flaws. But it still provided insights into human behavior using empirical approaches.

While not every recipe is perfect, each of these studies ultimately gave psychology richer ingredients for understanding the human experience. The scientific method isn't infallible, but it does provide a systematic means of testing theories and discovering knowledge - one delicious bite at a time!

Chapter 6: Treading with Care: The Ethics of Exploration in Psychology

Imagine you're invited to a magic show. The magician promises a spectacle, but under one condition: you must participate in one of the acts. Would you agree without knowing more? What if the act could be potentially harmful or embarrassing? Like magic, the world of psychological research can be mesmerizing, but it comes with its own set of responsibilities. Let's delve into the ethical principles that ensure research is not only enlightening but also respectful and safe.

Designing with Dignity: Ethical Considerations

Picture an architect designing a building. Beyond aesthetics, they must ensure the structure is safe for those inside. Similarly, when psychologists design research, they must ensure it's safe for participants.

This means studies should avoid causing harm—whether it's physical, emotional, or mental. For instance, if a researcher is studying stress, they can't put someone under extreme distress just to observe them. The well-being of the participant always comes first.

The Power of Choice: Informed Consent

Let's return to our magic show. Before participating in any act, you'd want to know what's involved, right? This principle is even more crucial in research. Informed consent means that participants have a clear understanding of the study, its purpose, what's expected of them, any potential risks, and their rights—including the right to leave the study at any time. It's all about ensuring participants are in the driver's seat, making informed decisions about their involvement.

Guarding Secrets: Confidentiality and Privacy

We all have secrets or personal details we'd rather keep private. In research, participants might share intimate details about their lives, feelings, or experiences. It's the researcher's duty to protect this information, ensuring it remains confidential. This often means that data is stored securely, and any identifying details are removed. It's like entrusting someone with a precious item, knowing they'll safeguard it with care.

The Twist in the Tale: Deception and Debriefing

Sometimes, to get genuine reactions, researchers might need to hide the true purpose of a study or provide misleading information. Think of it like a plot twist in a movie—it's necessary for the story.

However, this can't come at the expense of participants' well-being. If deception is used, it must be justified. Furthermore, once the study is over, participants are "debriefed." This means they're told the true nature of the study and the reasons behind the deception. It's like revealing the magic trick once it's over, ensuring everyone's in on the secret.

Embarking on a journey of discovery in psychology is exhilarating. However, like any voyage, it's essential to navigate with a compass of ethical responsibility. By ensuring research is conducted with care, respect, and transparency, psychology continues to shine a light on the human experience, enriching our understanding while upholding the dignity of all involved.

Chapter 7: Spicing Up the Scientific Method

Baking isn't just about following a recipe - it's also about tweaking and improving techniques. The scientific process also benefits from modifications over time. Peer review and replication are two key ways that psychologists refine their research recipes:

The Importance of Peer Review

Before publishing a recipe, chefs will often ask other experts to critique it. This provides an objective perspective. Similarly, scientists submit their work to peer review by the wider field. Colleagues scrutinize the methods and results to ensure quality.

Replication in Psychological Research

Recipes should consistently produce the same product. If others can't recreate it, something's not right. Replicating studies is a core scientific principle for psychology too. Repeating experiments helps confirm results were not merely coincidental.

Recent Replication Crises in Psychology

Lately, the field has realized that some of its recipes are not as reliable as thought. When recreating influential studies, psychologists have struggled to reproduce original findings, indicating issues in the original methodology. Just like an unreliable recipe, this signals that improvements in the scientific process are needed.

Peer review and replication are like getting your recipe tasted by other master chefs - it makes the end result more refined. While criticism can be hard to swallow, incorporating feedback leads to better food...or in this case, better science! The scientific method will keep evolving, but careful scrutiny by the field itself makes it a more trustworthy recipe in the long run.

Chapter 8: The Modern Tapestry: Today's Landscape of Psychological Inquiry

Imagine gazing at a vibrant, ever-changing skyline. Buildings that were once the epitome of modernity now stand beside dazzling new structures, each representing a leap in innovation and design. This ever-evolving skyline mirrors the exciting landscape of contemporary psychology. With new tools in hand and horizons expanding, today's psychological researchers are pushing the boundaries of understanding more than ever before. Let's take a tour of this dynamic terrain.

The New Toolkit: Technologies and Methods

Remember the days when maps were paper-based, and letters took weeks to reach their destination? Just as technology has revolutionized our daily lives, it's also reshaping psychology.

Brain imaging tools, like MRI machines, now allow researchers to peek into the human brain in action, observing which regions light up during different tasks or emotions. It's a bit like having a backstage pass to the most intricate performance!

Moreover, with the internet's rise, online surveys and experiments have become increasingly popular. Researchers can now reach people across the globe, gathering data more quickly and from diverse groups.

Fresh Horizons: Emerging Fields and Their Approaches

As the tools of psychology evolve, so do its areas of exploration. Let's explore some new neighborhoods in the sprawling city of psychology:

Positive Psychology: Instead of focusing only on disorders or problems, this field explores what makes life worth living. It studies happiness, resilience, and human strengths. Think of it as understanding the ingredients for a fulfilling life.

Cyberpsychology: As we spend more of our lives online, psychologists are keen to understand how digital realms affect our behavior, relationships, and well-being. From social media to virtual reality, this field delves into our digital selves.

Neuroplasticity: This exciting area studies how the brain can change and adapt over time. It's a bit like discovering that an old building can be renovated and transformed into something entirely new!

Gazing into the Crystal Ball: Future Directions

The journey of discovery is endless. As contemporary psychology stands on the shoulders of past giants, it also looks ahead, envisioning a future filled with promise.

One direction is the increasing fusion of psychology with genetics, understanding how our genes influence behavior and mental processes. Moreover, as artificial intelligence and machine learning grow, psychology will play a crucial role in understanding human-machine interactions and ensuring technology caters to human well-being.

Furthermore, as global challenges like climate change or pandemics emerge, psychology will be pivotal in understanding human behavior in these contexts and finding solutions that consider mental and emotional well-being.

The world of contemporary psychology is like a bustling, vibrant city, filled with innovation, exploration, and promise. With new tools, emerging fields, and an eye on the future, the journey of understanding the human mind and behavior is more thrilling than ever. As we marvel at today's discoveries, we also eagerly anticipate the breakthroughs of tomorrow.

Chapter 9: The Far Reach of Recipes

So far we've explored how the scientific method recipe whips up psychological insights. But this reliable formula has applications way beyond just psychology:

The Interdisciplinary Reach of the Scientific Method

Cooking techniques can be adapted across cuisines. Similar core methods yield results whether you're baking bread or grilling meat. The scientific method also extends far beyond psychology, underpinning knowledge in the natural sciences, social sciences, and more. Its ubiquity highlights its versatility.

Application of Psychological Scientific Methods in Other Fields

Unique recipes can provide inspiration beyond their original context. For example, molecular gastronomy has influenced mainstream cooking. Innovative research designs developed in psychology have also been applied in other fields like business and political science. Scientists are always borrowing good ideas from each other!

The Impact of Psychological Research on Society

A new recipe that takes off can transform home kitchens. Findings from psychology permeate our everyday lives too. Insights on human thinking and behavior influence everything from education to public policy to marketing. Like a popular recipe, robust psychological science spreads widely through society.

At the end of the day, the scientific method is a tried-and-true formula that allows understanding to rise and grow - from the oven of a single mind to kitchens everywhere. While fine-tuned over time, the core ingredients remain solid. Following the recipe of science means progress for not just psychology, but for collective human knowledge.

Chapter 10: Journey's End: Reflections on the Scientific Method in Psychology

Picture standing on a mountaintop, taking in the breathtaking panorama of the path you've traveled, the valleys crossed, and the peaks conquered. Our exploration of the scientific method in psychology has been much like this journey - filled with insights, discoveries, and moments of awe. As we pause to reflect, let's consider the immense power of this method, its inherent limitations, and its pivotal role in understanding the intricate tapestry of the human psyche.

The Dual-Edged Sword: Power and Limitations

The scientific method, with its structured approach and rigorous testing, has been like a beacon, guiding researchers through the complex maze of human behavior and thought. Its strength lies in its systematic nature - observing, hypothesizing, testing, and concluding. This method provides a pathway to glean insights that are not just based on mere opinions or anecdotes, but on tangible, observable evidence.

However, like any tool, it isn't without its limitations. Human behavior is incredibly complex and influenced by a myriad of factors. While the scientific method strives for objectivity, it's essential to remember that studies often capture a snapshot of a moment in time, under specific conditions. The real world, with its ever-changing dynamics, can sometimes be more fluid than controlled experimental settings.

The Heartbeat of Psychological Inquiry

Why do we dream? What drives us to love, to fear, to aspire? These are age-old questions, ones that have intrigued humanity for centuries. The scientific method in psychology is our best tool for seeking answers.

Without this method, psychology would be a field of mere speculation. It provides a structure, a framework, to delve deep into the human mind's mysteries. By observing, testing, and analyzing, researchers can move beyond superficial observations to uncover the underlying mechanisms that drive our emotions, behaviors, and thoughts.

Final Musings: Looking Back and Forging Ahead

Our journey through the landscape of the scientific method in psychology has been enlightening. We've ventured through history, explored key concepts, and witnessed the method's contemporary evolution. Along the way, we've seen its profound impact, from understanding basic human behaviors to addressing some of society's most pressing challenges.

As we stand at this journey's conclusion, it's clear that the scientific method is more than just a set of steps. It's a philosophy, a commitment to seeking truth with rigor, curiosity, and integrity. And while we've come a long way in our understanding, the horizon is vast, with many more mysteries awaiting discovery.

In the end, the quest to understand ourselves and others is perhaps one of the most profound journeys we can embark upon. With the scientific method as our compass, the possibilities are limitless.

About Freudian Trips

Welcome to Freudian Trips, your dedicated platform for diving deep into the world of psychology. We are more than just a YouTube channel or a book publisher. We are a beacon of enlightenment, making complex psychological concepts accessible and engaging for all.

Our YouTube channel is a rich repository of psychology made simple. We take the profound and often complex ideas from the world of psychology and break them down into digestible, easy-to-understand content. From the foundational theories of Freud to the cognitive insights of Piaget, we cover a broad spectrum of psychological schools and thoughts, making psychology accessible to everyone, regardless of their background or prior knowledge.

As a book publisher, we take the same approach, transforming intricate psychological theories into comprehensible narratives. Our books are not just collections of words, but vessels of wisdom that make psychology approachable and relatable. We believe that psychology should not be confined to academic circles, but should be available to all who seek to understand the human mind and behavior.

At Freudian Trips, we believe in the power of curiosity and the pursuit of knowledge. We are here to stoke the fires of your curiosity, to guide you on your intellectual journey, and to help you navigate the fascinating world of psychology.

If you are someone who is not afraid to question, to explore, and to learn, then you are in the right place. Join us on this journey of exploration, as we make psychology easy to understand, one concept at a time.

Be sure to visit our Youtube channel at: www.freudiantrips.com/youtube

You can also visit us on the web at www.freudiantrips.com

Welcome to The Freudian Trip community. Stay curious. Stay enlightened.